REWARDS

Reading Excellence: Word Attack & Rate Development Strategies

Multisyllabic Word Reading Strategies

Student Book

Anita L. Archer, Ph.D.

Mary M. Gleason, Ph.D.

Vicky Vachon, Ph.D.

Assisted by

Johnathan King

Pat Pielaet

 SOPRIS WEST™ EDUCATIONAL SERVICES

A CAMBIUM LEARNING COMPANY

BOSTON, MA • LONGMONT, CO

Copyright 2006 by Sopris West Educational Services
All rights reserved.

19 20 21   HPS   15 14 13 12

Teacher's Guide ISBN 13 Digit: 978-1-59318-551-0
Teacher's Guide ISBN 10 Digit: 1-59318-551-0
Student Book ISBN 13 Digit: 978-1-59318-552-7
Student Book ISBN 10 Digit: 1-59318-552-9
Packet of Overhead Transparencies ISBN 13 Digit: 978-1-59318-553-4
Packet of Overhead Transparencies ISBN 10 Digit: 1-59318-553-7
116353/3-12

Cover images: ©Brand X Pictures, ©Masterfile Royalty Free,
©Inmagine, ©Comstock Royalty Free/Fotosearch

No portion of this book may be reproduced or transmitted in any form or by any means, electronic or
mechanical, including photocopying or recording, or by any information storage and retrieval system,
without the express written permission of the publisher.

Printed in the United States of America

Published and Distributed by

Sopris West™
EDUCATIONAL SERVICES

A Cambium Learning Company

4093 Specialty Place ■ Longmont, Colorado 80504
(303) 651-2829 ■ www.sopriswest.com

Contents

Letter to Students from the *REWARDS* Authors

Dear Students,

Welcome to the *REWARDS* program. This program will teach you how to read long words having two to eight parts. As you proceed through the grades, more and more of the words contain many parts. These longer words are particularly important because they often carry the meaning in content area textbooks.

In addition to learning strategies for reading long words, you will also be building your reading rate or fluency. As you know from your own experience, it is not only important to read words accurately but quickly. As you become a more fluent reader, you will be able to complete your reading assignments more quickly and will find recreational reading more enjoyable.

Hundreds of students have used this program in the past and found it to strengthen their reading skills. We hope that you experience the same gains and have ever increasing confidence in your reading.

May you reap all the REWARDS of this program.

Anita Archer
Mary Gleason
Vicky Vachon

Activity A: **Oral Activity—Blending Word Parts Into Words**

Activity B: **Vowel Combinations**

ay (say)	ai (rain)

Activity C: **Vowel Conversions**

a	i

Activity D: **Reading Parts of Real Words**

1.	tain	mit	stract	mid
2.	ta *	id	vict	la *
3.	cay	dain	tri *	tract
4.	hap	trast	mand	trict

Activity E: **Underlining Vowels in Words**

1.	pathway	waist	pigtail
2.	maintain	midday	rapid
3.	backspin	haystack	milkman
4.	railway	panic	strain
5.	midway	mailman	mainsail

Activity F: **Oral Activity—Correcting Close Approximations Using Context**

Activity G: **Prefixes and Suffixes**

disagree	dis
mistake	mis
absent	ab
addition	ad

Activity H: **Circling Prefixes and Suffixes**

1.	misfit	dismiss	abstract
2.	dash	misplay	addict
3.	disband	misprint	disclaim
4.	dismay	mint	distract
5.	display	admit	mislaid
6.	aim	district	disdain
7.	abstain	mishap	miscast

Activity I: **Vocabulary**

a. a person who is a wrong fit for a group of people

(Line 1, Activity H) _____

b. to not claim (Line 3, Activity H) _____

c. laid down in the wrong place (Line 5, Activity H)

_____

Special Vocabulary

1. distract—If someone takes your attention away from what you are doing, they <u>distract</u> you.

2. dismay—When you feel discouraged about a problem, you feel <u>dismay</u>.

Activity J: **Spelling Dictation**

1.	2.
3.	4.

Lesson 2

Activity A: **Oral Activity—Blending Word Parts Into Words**

Activity B: **Vowel Combinations**

au
(sauce)

1.	au	ai	ay	au
2.	ay	au	ai	au

Activity C: **Vowel Conversions**

a	i

Activity D: **Reading Parts of Real Words**

1.	dit	rai	fant	bla *
2.	hib	tinct	ti *	hab
3.	pact	sist	naut	bi *
4.	flict	val	vic	jaun

Activity E: **Underlining Vowels in Words**

1.	ransack	vault	raisin
2.	victim	waistband	fraud
3.	timid	fault	valid
4.	jaunt	claim	cause
5.	captain	audit	candid

Activity F: **Oral Activity—Correcting Close Approximations Using Context**

Activity G: **Prefixes and Suffixes**

(in)complete	in
(im)mature	im
(com)pare	com
(con)tinue	con

Prefixes

1.	in	com	dis	mis	im	con
2.	im	ad	con	in	ab	com

Activity H: **Circling Prefixes and Suffixes**

1.	insist	commit	imprint
2.	camp	inlaid	consist
3.	distinct	inhabit	dim
4.	convict	ingrain	implant
5.	complain	impact	cash
6.	inflict	command	mislay
7.	impair	contrast	infant

Activity I: **Vocabulary**

a. **laid into a surface, such as a table** (Line 2, Activity H)

_____

b. **something planted in the body during surgery**

(Line 4, Activity H) _____

c. **to lay down in the wrong place** (Line 6, Activity H)

_____

Special Vocabulary

1. contrast—When you show or tell the differences between two things, you <u>contrast</u> those things.

2. insist—If you speak very strongly about something, you <u>insist</u>.

Activity J: **Spelling Dictation**

1.	2.
3.	4.

Activity A: **Oral Activity—Blending Word Parts Into Words**

Activity B: **Vowel Combinations**

er	ir	ur
(her)	(bird)	(turn)

1.	ir	ay	au	ur
2.	ai	ir	er	au

Activity C: **Vowel Conversions**

o	a	i

Activity D: **Reading Parts of Real Words**

1.	cur	tro *	vas	serv
2.	to *	surd	bliz	pris
3.	ver	dom	der	plaint
4.	turb	laun	vi *	strict

Activity E: **Underlining Vowels in Words**

1.	curtail	birthday	turn
2.	auto *	astronaut *	random
3.	launch	verdict	vitamin *
4.	birdbath	turban	whirlwind
5.	auburn	server	taunt

Activity F: **Oral Activity—Correcting Close Approximations Using Context**

Activity G: **Prefixes and Suffixes**

belong	be	prevent	pre
depart	de	protect	pro
return	re		

Prefixes

1.	be	com	pro	ab	dis	de
2.	pro	re	mis	con	pre	be
3.	de	pre	com	ad	pro	re

Activity H: **Circling Prefixes and Suffixes**

1.	prefer	disturb	canvas
2.	proclaim	betray	defraud
3.	behind	complaint	decay
4.	confirm	detail	reclaim
5.	absurd	prepay	restrain
6.	prohibit	distant	behold
7.	restrict	invalid	prison

Activity I: **Vocabulary**

a.   **to claim again** (Line 4, Activity H) _____

b.   **to pay before you get something** (Line 5, Activity H)

_____

c.   **not valid or not true** (Line 7, Activity H)

_____

Special Vocabulary

1.   prefer—If you like something better than something else, you <u>prefer</u> that thing.

2.   absurd—When something is so untrue or so silly that we laugh at it, we could say it is <u>absurd</u>.

Activity J: **Spelling Dictation**

1.	2.
3.	4.

Lesson 4

Activity A: **Oral Activity—Blending Word Parts Into Words**

Activity B: **Vowel Combinations**

ar	or
(farm)	(torn)

1.	or	au	ar	ai
2.	ir	ar	ay	or

Activity C: **Vowel Conversions**

a	o	i

Activity D: **Reading Parts of Real Words**

1.	gar	na *	hol	fraid
2.	lert	cos	po *	pert
3.	mer	bor	zard	ber
4.	tor	lin	ner	sorb

Activity E: **Underlining Vowels in Words**

1.	blizzard	holiday	haunt
2.	mermaid	shortstop	partner
3.	northern	cargo *	hardship
4.	border	vermin	overhaul *
5.	garland	backyard	barbershop

Activity F: **Oral Activity—Correcting Close Approximations Using Context**

Activity G: **Prefixes and Suffixes**

(per)mit	per
(un)fair	un
(a)bove	a

Prefixes

1.	per	con	de	un	in	a
2.	con	a	dis	im	ad	pro
3.	pre	com	mis	per	ab	re
4.	un	con	be	per	com	a

Activity H: **Circling Prefixes and Suffixes**

1.	constrict	deprogram	cannon
2.	across	misinform	repay
3.	deform	unfit	unafraid
4.	absorb	perform	preserve
5.	perturb	impart	prefix
6.	record	alert	discard
7.	unchain	persist	prolong

Activity I: **Vocabulary**

a.	to give the wrong information (Line 2, Activity H)
	_____
b.	not fit or not healthy (Line 3, Activity H)
	_____
c.	to remove from chains (Line 7, Activity H)
	_____

Special Vocabulary

1. persist—When you keep working on something or keep trying to do something, you <u>persist</u> at that thing.
2. discard—When you throw something away, you <u>discard</u> it.

Activity J: **Spelling Dictation**

1.	2.
3.	4.

Activity A: **Oral Activity—Blending Word Parts Into Words**

Activity B: **Vowel Combinations**

a - e (make)	o - e (hope)	i - e (side)	e - e (Pete)	u - e (use)

1.	a - e	ai	au	or	e - e
2.	er	au	o - e	ar	ur
3.	i - e	u - e	ay	o - e	a - e

Activity C: **Vowel Conversions**

u	i	a	o

Activity D: **Reading Parts of Real Words**

1.	treme	clude	do *	scribe
2.	tume	trate	gust	mur
3.	stile	pede	pau	lete
4.	struct	mote	larm	so *

Activity E: **Underlining Vowels in Words**

1.	costume	timberline	turnstile
2.	stampede	autumn	backbone
3.	shipmate	maximum	sunstroke
4.	frustrate	marlin	murmur
5.	popcorn	tornado	obsolete
		* *	*

Activity F: **Oral Activity—Correcting Close Approximations Using Context**

Activity G: **Prefixes and Suffixes**

(ex)port	ex
(en)list	en

Prefixes

1.	be	en	com	per	dis	ex
2.	con	un	im	de	ab	pre
3.	ex	re	com	in	mis	in
4.	a	com	en	ex	con	ad

Activity H: **Circling Prefixes and Suffixes**

1.	explain	disgust	reconstruct
2.	promote	unalike	berate
3.	combine	alarm	exact
4.	entire	readjust	impose
5.	enthrone	unpaid	misbehave
6.	prescribe	exclude	entail
7.	conclude	advise	extreme

Activity I: **Vocabulary**

a. **to construct or build again** (Line 1, Activity H)

_____

b. **to adjust or change again** (Line 4, Activity H)

_____

c. **not paid** (Line 5, Activity H) _____

Special Vocabulary

1. exclude—when you leave someone or something out of a group, you <u>exclude</u> them.

2. entire—If you are talking about the whole group, and all the members of that group, you are talking about the <u>entire</u> group.

Activity J: **Spelling Dictation**

1.	2.
3.	4.

Lesson 6

Activity A: **Oral Activity—Blending Word Parts Into Words**

Activity B: **Vowel Combinations**

oi	oy
(boil)	(boy)

1.	au	oy	a - e	i - e	or
2.	oi	ar	ay	ai	oy
3.	o - e	er	ur	oi	ir

Activity C: **Vowel Conversions**

o	u	i	a

Activity D: **Reading Word Parts**

1.	moil	ster	mi*	tise
2.	plete	trude	trins	grad
3.	cor	gard	loi	crim
4.	frant	stroy	poi	cott

Activity E: **Underlining Vowels in Words**

1.	turmoil	corduroy	boycott
2.	corrode	void	spoilsport
3.	barter	poison	joyride
4.	pauper	oyster	hoist
5.	loiter	launder	ordain

Activity F: **Oral Activity—Correcting Close Approximations Using Context**

Activity G: **Prefixes and Suffixes**

bird(s)	s	use(less)	less
runn(ing)	ing	kind(ness)	ness
land(ed)	ed	athlet(ic)	ic
regul(ate)	ate		

Prefixes

1.	ex	con	in	per	pro	pre
2.	un	a	mis	en	com	re

Suffixes

3.	less	ing	ate	ness	ate	ic
4.	ate	less	ness	ic	ing	less

Activity H: **Circling Prefixes and Suffixes**

1.	extrinsic	hardness	hopelessness
2.	demanded	regardless	alarming
3.	dominates	relaxing	carelessness
4.	happiness	classic	captivates
5.	discriminate	frantic	rejoin
6.	graduate	destroy	fantastic
7.	softness	departed	completeness

Activity I: **Vocabulary**

a.   the state of being without hope (Line 1, Activity H)

_____

b.   the quality of being soft (Line 7, Activity H)

_____

c.   the condition of being complete (Line 7, Activity H)

_____

Special Vocabulary

1.   discriminate—When people treat another person or group differently because of their race or religion, they <u>discriminate</u> against that person or group.

2.   destroy—When you wreck something or break it into pieces, you <u>destroy</u> it.

Activity J: **Spelling Dictation**

1.	2.
3.	4.

Activity A: **Oral Activity—Blending Word Parts Into Words**

Activity B: **Vowel Combinations**

ee
(deep)

1.	ee	ar	au	ur	oy
2.	u - e	or	ee	o - e	i - e
3.	ir	oi	ai	ay	ee

Activity C: **Vowel Conversions**

e	o	a	u	i

Activity D: **Reading Parts of Real Words**

1.	slo *	spect	sim	fif
2.	trode	auth	ston	duct
3.	pes	hudd	hend	lorn
4.	tex	blem	flor	fe *

Activity E: **Underlining Vowels in Words**

1.	streetcar	uniform *	fifteenth
2.	forget	textile	sweepstake
3.	freedom	forest	canteen
4.	female *	leftover *	forlorn
5.	penmanship	homeland	benefit

Activity F: **Oral Activity—Correcting Close Approximations Using Context**

Activity G: **Prefixes and Suffixes**

self(ish)	ish	bigg(est)	est
art(ist)	ist	real(ism)	ism

Prefixes

1.	ab	a	pre	en	con	com
2.	per	con	un	ex	ad	a

Suffixes

3.	ish	ate	ism	ness	est	ate
4.	ism	ic	ing	less	ish	ist

Activity H: **Circling Prefixes and Suffixes**

1. alarmist	vanish	astonishing
2. punish	unselfish	interested
3. pessimism	comprehends	famish
4. respected	untrusting	heroism
5. intrude	conducted	optimism
6. humanist	advertise	smartest
7. disarm	florist	blemish

Activity I: **Vocabulary**

a.   not selfish (Line 2, Activity H) _____

b.   the most smart (Line 6, Activity H)

_____

c.   to remove arms or weapons (Line 7, Activity H)

_____

Special Vocabulary

1.   optimism—When you expect the best results, you have <u>optimism</u>.

2.   pessimism—When you expect the worst results, you have <u>pessimism</u>.

Activity J: **Spelling Dictation**

1.	2.
3.	4.

Lesson 8

Activity A: **Oral Activity—Blending Word Parts Into Words**

Activity B: **Vowel Combinations**

oa	ou
(boat)	(loud)

1.	oa	oi	au	ou	i - e
2.	ee	or	oy	ay	oa
3.	ou	er	ar	a - e	ai

The Other Sound of C

cent	city	cycle
space	civil	cyclone
cellar	pencil	fancy

Activity C: **Vowel Conversions**

a	i	o	u	e

Activity D: **Reading Parts of Real Words**

1.	cide	pa *	cen	ploy
2.	cess	sid	cit	fau
3.	loy	plode	spec	sir
4.	thir	sus	lec	pi *

Activity E: **Underlining Vowels in Words**

1.	southwestern	cloudburst	seventeen
2.	carload	railroad	coach
3.	roadside	electrode	playground
4.	faucet	spellbound	northwestern
5.	coatrack	greenhouse	census

Activity F: **Oral Activity—Correcting Close Approximations Using Context**

Activity G: **Prefixes and Suffixes**

care**ful**	ful	farm**er**	er
fin**al**	al	invent**or**	or

Prefixes

1.	com	de	en	mis	per	con
2.	ex	a	pro	pre	com	im

Suffixes

3.	ful	ist	er	est	or	al
4.	al	or	ate	ful	ic	ism

Activity H: **Circling Prefixes and Suffixes**

1.	loyalist	employer	percent
2.	consider	sailor	proposal
3.	author	consumers	respectful
4.	advertiser	personal	historical
5.	arrival	explode	cinder
6.	spectator	ungrateful	unfortunate
7.	untruthful	abnormal	successful

Activity I: **Vocabulary**

a.   being full of respect (Line 3, Activity H)

_____

b.   relating to a particular person (Line 4, Activity H)

_____

c.   being full of success (Line 7, Activity H)

_____

Special Vocabulary
1.   unfortunate—When you are not lucky, you are <u>unfortunate</u>.
2.   spectator—When you watch a sporting event, a parade, or a play, you are a <u>spectator</u>.

Activity J: **Spelling Dictation**

1.	2.
3.	4.

Lesson 9

Activity A: **Oral Activity—Blending Word Parts Into Words**

Activity B: **Vowel Combinations**

ow
(low) (down)

1.	oa	ow	au	ay	oy
2.	ow	er	a - e	oi	or
3.	ou	ee	ai	ow	ar

The Other Sound of C		
cent	city	cycle
price	citrus	lacy
center	decide	cyclops

Activity C: **Vowel Conversions**

a	e	o	i	u

Activity D: **Reading Parts of Real Words**

1.	dow	te *	gret	gre *
2.	ceed	cel	plow	sence
3.	laud	flow	har	strugg
4.	semb	civ	mar	cer

Activity E: **Underlining Vowels in Words**

1.	pillow	chowder	roadway
2.	succeed	elbow	cinch
3.	flowerpot	willow	outgrow
4.	snowplow	embrace	sundown
5.	thirteenth	shallow	windowpane

Activity F: **Oral Activity—Correcting Close Approximations Using Context**

Activity G: **Prefixes and Suffixes**

cour(age)	age
crad(le)	le

Prefixes

1.	mis	be	pro	un	com	dis
2.	con	ex	pro	per	a	con

Suffixes

3.	age	ful	ist	al	or	le
4.	less	le	ate	age	est	ism

Activity H: **Circling Prefixes and Suffixes**

1.	manage	computers	struggle
2.	reconsider	priceless	programmer
3.	mishandle	absence	regretful
4.	successor	bemoan	mileage
5.	elevator	harvested	huddle
6.	barbarism	unfaithful	shortage
7.	resemble	sausage	entertainers

Activity I: **Vocabulary**

a.   a person who programs computers (Line 2, Activity H)

_____

b.   not faithful or not loyal (Line 6, Activity H)

_____

c.   people who entertain others (Line 7, Activity H)

_____

Special Vocabulary

1.   reconsider—If you carefully think about an idea again, you <u>reconsider</u> the idea.

2.   resemble—If you look like or act like another person, you <u>resemble</u> that person.

Activity J: **Spelling Dictation**

1.	2.
3.	4.

Lesson 10

Activity A: **Oral Activity—Blending Word Parts Into Words**

Activity B: **Vowel Combinations**

ow
(low) (down)

1.	ow	oa	ow	ir	ar
2.	oi	or	au	ay	ou
3.	ou	ow	ur	ai	oy

The Other Sound of G		
gentle	gist	gypsy
gem	giraffe	energy
change	magic	gym

Activity C: **Vowel Conversions**

u	a	e	o	i

Activity D: **Reading Parts of Real Words**

1.	blow	il	loin	ple *
2.	gen	pow	shad	germ
3.	sault	gant	mo *	tec
4.	show	blige	nov	cau

Activity E: **Underlining Vowels in Words**

1.	rainbow	margin	township
2.	shadow	lifeboat	oblige
3.	boatload	germfree	downtown
4.	snowflake	outgrowth	downhill
5.	sirloin	cowboy	marshmallow

Activity F: **Oral Activity—Correcting Close Approximations Using Context**

Activity G: **Prefixes and Suffixes**

| ac(tion) | tion | atten(tive) | tive |
| discus(sion) | sion | expen(sive) | sive |

Prefixes

| 1. | ex | com | re | im | a | con |
| 2. | un | pro | ab | de | com | en |

Suffixes

| 3. | tion | age | or | sive | le | sion |
| 4. | tive | sion | ful | al | tion | tive |

Activity H: **Circling Prefixes and Suffixes**

1.	expansive	protection	permissive
2.	novelist	repulsive	civilization
3.	percussionist	gigantic	invasion
4.	postage	expression	caution
5.	refusal	completion	regenerate
6.	conditional	effective	demonstrations
7.	unintentional	panelist	professional

Activity I: **Vocabulary**

---

a.   the act of protecting from harm (Line 1, Activity H)

_____

b.   the act of expressing oneself (Line 4, Activity H)

_____

c.   the act of refusing (Line 5, Activity H)

_____

Special Vocabulary

1.   repulsive—When you really dislike something or are really bothered by it, it would be <u>repulsive</u>.

2.   permissive—If parents gave their children too much freedom, the parents would be <u>permissive</u>.

Activity J: **Spelling Dictation**

1.	2.
3.	4.

Lesson 11

Activity A: Oral Activity—Blending Word Parts Into Words

Activity B: Vowel Combinations

oo
(moon) (book)

1.	oo	au	oi	ow	ar
2.	oa	e - e	ou	oo	ai
3.	oy	oo	ee	ur	ow

The Other Sound of G

gentle	gist	gypsy
gerbil	ginger	trilogy
urgent	engineer	gymnast

Activity C: Vowel Conversions

e	u	i	a	o

Activity D: **Reading Parts of Real Words**

1.	hood	vol	jur	foot
2.	fec	tam	plex	lar
3.	co *	va *	crow	bil
4.	roon	pend	toon	gree

Activity E: **Underlining Vowels in Words**

1.	cartoon	toothpick	igloo
2.	footprint	monsoon	riverbank
3.	cookbook	shampoo	showboat
4.	sagebrush	fishhook	loophole
5.	woodshed	macaroon	boomerang

Activity F: **Oral Activity—Correcting Close Approximations Using Context**

Activity G: **Prefixes and Suffixes**

| thirst(y) | y | mission(ary) | ary |
| safe(ly) | ly | odd(ity) | ity |

Prefixes					
1. in	com	pro	a	ex	dis
2. a	pre	en	un	con	per

Suffixes					
3. sion	ary	ate	ly	le	sive
4. y	ism	ary	age	ity	al

Activity H: **Circling Prefixes and Suffixes**

1. precaution	dictionary	celery
2. injury	dismissal	belabor
3. disability	absurdity	complexity
4. grocery	energetic	voluntary
5. nationally	similarity	relatively
6. adhesive	disloyal	perfectionist
7. personality	intensive	contaminate

Activity I: **Vocabulary**

a. caution taken before doing something (Line 1, Activity H)

_____

b. not loyal (Line 6, Activity H)

_____

c. a person who wants perfection (Line 6, Activity H)

_____

Special Vocabulary

1. contaminate—If we pollute or make something unclean, we contaminate it.

2. voluntary—When you do something that you don't have to do but just want to do it, it would be a voluntary act.

Activity J: **Spelling Dictation**

1.	2.
3.	4.

Lesson 12

Activity A: **Oral Activity—Blending Word Parts Into Words**

Activity B: **Vowel Combinations**

oo
(moon) (book)

1.	ai	oo	ay	er	ow
2.	ar	oi	ee	oo	oy
3.	ow	or	au	ir	oo

Activity C: **Vowel Conversions**

o	a	u	e	i

Activity D: **Reading Parts of Real Words**

1.	roof	chow	scrap	dif
2.	cite	kan	doc	fir
3.	rac	aut	room	ges
4.	struc	coon	fect	pli

*

Activity E: **Underlining Vowels in Words**

1.	raccoon	scapegoat	uproot
2.	outlook	fluke	boyhood
3.	rooftop	scrapbook	firstborn
4.	balloon	classroom	girlhood
5.	toothbrush	kangaroo	schoolyard

Activity F: **Oral Activity—Correcting Close Approximations Using Context**

Activity G: **Prefixes and Suffixes**

dorm(ant)	ant
persist(ent)	ent
argu(ment)	ment

Prefixes

1.	dis	pro	ex	ad	en	com
2.	pre	con	a	in	per	re

Suffixes

3.	ant	ity	ly	age	tive	ment
4.	ary	le	ent	y	tion	ant

Activity H: **Circling Prefixes and Suffixes**

1.	complimentary	continent	racism
2.	different	documentary	challenging
3.	servant	passage	suggestive
4.	cartoonist	permanent	assistant
5.	excitement	princely	examination
6.	independently	enjoyment	entertainment
7.	disinfectant	unemployment	construction

Activity I: **Vocabulary**

a.   **a person who serves** (Line 3, Activity H)

_____

b.   **a person who assists or helps** (Line 4, Activity H)

_____

c.   **the act of enjoying** (Line 6, Activity H)

_____

Special Vocabulary

1.   permanent—If something is meant to last forever without changing, it is <u>permanent</u>.

2.   examination—Another word for test is <u>examination</u>.

Activity J: **Spelling Dictation**

1.	2.
3.	4.

Activity A: **Oral Activity—Blending Word Parts Into Words**

Activity B: **Vowel Combinations**

ea
(meat) (thread)

1.	au	ea	oo	oy	ai
2.	ow	ir	ou	or	oo
3.	a - e	oa	ea	i - e	ay
4.	ea	ee	ar	oo	oi

Activity C: **Vowel Conversions**

i	o	e	a	u

Activity D: **Reading Parts of Real Words**

1.	mead	fa *	steam	tend
2.	trow	ger	fid	gent
3.	mitt	meal	proof	tol
4.	port	nif	net	stead

Activity E: **Underlining Vowels in Words**

1.	steamboat	bedroom	streambed
2.	meadow	peanut	widespread
3.	showdown	streamline	meant
4.	seashell	headstrong	meantime
5.	oatmeal	daydream	gingerbread

Activity F: **Oral Activity—Correcting Close Approximations Using Context**

Activity G: **Prefixes and Suffixes**

disturb(ance)   ance

influ(ence)   ence

Prefixes

1.	a	con	en	pro	mis	re
2.	ex	im	per	ab	pre	com

Suffixes

3.	ity	ance	ism	ment	sive	ence
4.	ant	ary	ance	ate	ence	ly

Activity H: **Circling Prefixes and Suffixes**

1.	explanation	difference	dependence
2.	importance	fictional	refinance
3.	gently	endurance	baggage
4.	powerfully	confectionary	attendance
5.	admittance	intolerant	magnetism
6.	maintenance	misunderstand	confidence
7.	significance	performance	consistent

Activity I: **Vocabulary**

a.   in a manner that is powerful (Line 4, Activity H)

_____

b.   not tolerant; not willing to accept differences
(Line 5, Activity H)

_____

c.   thinking or acting in the same way again and
again (Line 7, Activity H)

_____

Special Vocabulary

1.   dependence—When someone has to do something for us, we have
<u>dependence</u> on that person.

2.   endurance—When you can do something for a very long time, you
have <u>endurance</u>.

Activity J: **Spelling Dictation**

1.	2.
3.	4.

Activity A: **Oral Activity—Blending Word Parts Into Words**

Activity B: **Vowel Combinations**

ea
(meat) (thread)

1.	ow	oa	ea	au	or
2.	ee	ar	er	o - e	oo
3.	ea	ou	oy	ay	au
4.	ow	ai	ir	oi	ea

Activity C: **Vowel Conversions**

u	o	a	i	e

Activity D: **Reading Parts of Real Words**

1.	thread	ca *	vel	break
2.	par	boon	tre *	fac
3.	tra *	phan	read	ven
4.	ves	clu *	ket	fes

Activity E: **Underlining Vowels in Words**

1.	peacock	threadbare	steamship
2.	breakfast	gemstone	moonbeam
3.	footpath	soybean	letterhead
4.	health	seamstress	sweatshirt
5.	seaweed	proofread	southeastern

Activity F: **Oral Activity—Correcting Close Approximations Using Context**

Activity G: **Prefixes and Suffixes**

fam(ous)	ous
pic(ture)	ture

Prefixes

1.	com	pre	mis	pro	im	per
2.	re	dis	con	dis	a	dis

Suffixes

3.	ous	ity	ary	ence	or	ture
4.	tion	ance	age	er	ture	ous

Activity H: **Circling Prefixes and Suffixes**

1.	marvelous	continuous	healthy
2.	inactive	literature	orphanage
3.	enormous	tremendous	absorbent
4.	departure	instructors	elementary
5.	excessive	conformity	vulture
6.	adventure	ineffective	confession
7.	investigation	inconclusive	identification

Activity I: **Vocabulary**

a.   given to excess or beyond what is necessary (Line 5,

Activity H) _____

b.   not effective because it doesn't work (Line 6, Activity H)

_____

c.   not having a conclusion or clear result (Line 7,

Activity H) _____

Special Vocabulary

1.   continuous—If something just keeps on going without stopping, it is <u>continuous</u>.

2.   investigation—When we really want to know something and we search for information about it, we are involved in an <u>investigation</u>.

Activity J: **Spelling Dictation**

1.	2.
3.	4.

Activity A: **Oral Activity—Blending Word Parts Into Words**

Activity B: **Vowel Combinations**

ea
(meat) (thread)

1.	ea	oo	oi	oa	ou
2.	or	au	ir	i - e	ow
3.	ee	a - e	ay	ea	er
4.	ur	ea	ai	oy	oo

Activity C: **Vowel Conversions**

e	u	i	a	o

Activity D: **Reading Parts of Real Words**

1.	round	sur	team	foil
2.	norm	scrip	tinc	flex
3.	poss	tin	cred	place
4.	fort	spons	vail	speak

Activity E: **Underlining Vowels in Words**

1.	teammate	headdress	marketplace
2.	monorail	tinfoil	reason
	*		
3.	seasick	surround	baboon
4.	bedspread	torpedo	downstream
		* *	
5.	bookcase	footstool	sunbeam

Activity F: **Oral Activity—Correcting Close Approximations Using Context**

Activity G: **Prefixes and Suffixes**

comfort(able)	able
revers(ible)	ible
memor(ize)	ize

Prefixes

1.	ex	pro	con	im	mis	per
2.	un	a	ab	com	in	en

Suffixes

3.	ize	able	ence	ous	ment	ible
4.	able	ance	ture	ant	ize	ary

Activity H: **Circling Prefixes and Suffixes**

1.	inconsistently	impossible	responsible
2.	predictable	available	civilize
3.	drinkable	normalize	descriptive
4.	laminate	inflexible	preventable
5.	incapable	incredible	legalize
6.	misunderstanding	enjoyable	sterilize
7.	department	reproduction	unconventional

Activity I: **Vocabulary**

a.   not possible (Line 1, Activity H)

_____

b.   able to be predicted or told ahead of time

(Line 2, Activity H) _____

c.   a wrong understanding (Line 6, Activity H)

_____

Special Vocabulary

1.   inconsistently—If you are not acting consistently or in the same way each time, you are behaving <u>inconsistently</u>.

2.   available—If you can get something or use something, it is <u>available</u>.

Activity J: **Spelling Dictation**

1.	2.
3.	4.

Activity A: Vowel Combinations Review

1.	au	er	☐ ea ☐	oa	e - e
2.	oi	ur	oy	ee	i - e
3.	☐ ow ☐	ay	u - e	☐ oo ☐	or

Activity B: Vowel Conversions Review

o	i	e	u	a

Activity C: Prefixes and Suffixes Review

	Prefixes				
1.	per	a	con	en	be
2.	mis	in	com	un	pro

	Suffixes				
3.	ance	tion	y	ture	ible
4.	able	ist	ity	ness	le
5.	ly	ment	ous	al	ent

Activity D: **Strategy Instruction**

1.	prevention	description
2.	estimate	unlucky
3.	excellence	redundant
4.	appearance	adversity
5.	community	enormity
6.	remainder	prediction

Activity E: **Strategy Practice**

1.	helplessness	distinction
2.	projector	numerous
3.	consultant	connection

Activity F: **Word Families**

A	**B**
prevent—to keep from happening	connect—to join or fasten together
prevents	connected
prevented	connecting
preventing	connection
prevention	reconnect
preventable	reconnecting
unpreventable	reconnection

Activity G: **Spelling Dictation**

1.	2.
3.	4.

Activity H: **Vocabulary**

a. not lucky (Activity D) _____

b. the result of predicting or making a guess
(Activity D) _____

c. the result of being connected (Activity E)

_____

Special Vocabulary
1. adversity—When you have many things go wrong in your life or you have many problems, you experience <u>adversity</u>.
2. estimate—If you guess an amount or number, you <u>estimate</u>.

Activity I: **Sentence Reading**

1. The consultant will help the people plan for the rock star's appearance.

2. The community felt great helplessness in the face of adversity.

3. The description of the art gallery made it sound quite marvelous.

4. The police department was awarded a medal of distinction for excellence in crime prevention.

5. The projector did not work because the connection was poor.

6. The students needed to estimate the remainder for the division problems.

7. The teacher laminated the remainder of the pictures so they would not be ruined.

8. The passage repeated the main points several times, making the last two pages very redundant.

9. The unlucky children were very upset with the enormity of the impossible task.

10. Numerous events in the community were halted because of the adversity.

Activity A: **Vowel Combinations Review**

1.	ir	or	oa	oo	ay
2.	u - e	ai	ar	ou	oy
3.	i - e	ow	ea	ur	oi

Activity B: **Vowel Conversions Review**

a	e	u	o	i

Activity C: **Prefixes and Suffixes Review**

Prefixes

1.	dis	ad	im	pre	ex
2.	de	re	ab	com	a

Suffixes

3.	less	ic	ing	ate	ish
4.	est	ary	ism	ful	or
5.	age	sion	ence	ent	ize

Activity D: **Strategy Instruction**

1.	temporary	perfection
2.	complaining	beginner
3.	suddenness	reduction
4.	pollution	productive
5.	observant	propeller
6.	extinction	mismanage

Activity E: **Strategy Practice**

1.	convertible	ignorance
2.	refreshments	amazingly
3.	unpredictable	promotion

Activity F: **Word Families**

A	**B**
predict—to tell about something before it happens	produce—to make something
predicts	production
predicted	productive
predicting	productivity
predictor	productiveness
prediction	reproduce
unpredictable	reproduction

Activity G: **Spelling Dictation**

1.	2.
3.	4.

Activity H: **Vocabulary**

a.   a person who is beginning something new (Activity D)

_____

b.   the state of being perfect (Activity D) _____

c.   not able to be predicted (Activity E) _____

Special Vocabulary

1.   productive—Someone who is <u>productive</u> is very successful at making or growing something.

2.   promotion—When a person has a job and gets an even better job in the same company, that person gets a <u>promotion</u>.

Activity I: **Sentence Reading**

1. He polished the convertible to perfection until it was sleek and shiny.

2. The propeller on the boat stopped with great suddenness.

3. The beginner was discouraged and began complaining about her friend's promotion.

4. The storms were unpredictable, so getting soaked was unpreventable.

5. Their ignorance of the effects of pollution on health was due to their complete lack of information.

6. His prediction regarding the reduction in pay discouraged the workers.

7. The observant walker moved down the slippery stairs with great caution.

8. Amazingly, the refreshments were prepared on time.

9. The furnishings were so exact that the room had a look of great distinction.

10. The suddenness with which he received the promotion surprised numerous other workers.

Lesson 18

Activity A: **Vowel Combinations Review**

1.	ea	a - e	e - e	au	ee
2.	oi	o - e	oo	oa	ow
3.	er	ir	ar	ai	ou

Activity B: **Vowel Conversions Review**

e	i	a	o	u

Activity C: **Prefixes and Suffixes Review**

Prefixes

1.	ab	in	con	pro	en
2.	re	com	ad	per	ex

Suffixes

3.	ism	ary	ize	able	ous
4.	ance	ent	ture	le	age
5.	tive	er	ence	sive	ment

Activity D: **Strategy Instruction**

1.	exceptionally	independence
2.	uncomfortable	surrender
3.	invention	expectation
4.	disposable	development

Activity E: **Strategy Practice**

1.	permanently	amusement
2.	utterance	suddenly
3.	impersonal	existence
4.	importantly	indifferent
5.	deformity	containers

Activity F: **Word Families**

A	**B**
invent—to make something that has never been made before	develop—to take something that has been invented and make it better
invents	developed
inventor	developer
invention	developing
inventive	development
reinvent	developmental
reinvention	developmentally

Activity G: **Spelling Dictation**

1.	2.
3.	4.

Activity H: **Vocabulary**

a.   the act of developing or making something (Activity D)

_____

b.   not personal (Activity E) _____

c.   the condition of being deformed (Activity E)

_____

Special Vocabulary

1.   expectation—When you think that something might happen, you have an <u>expectation</u>.

2.   utterance—When you say something, the spoken words are called an <u>utterance</u>.

Activity I: **Sentence Reading**

1.   Reproduction allows the ongoing existence of plants and animals.

2.   Mario was so famished, he suddenly grabbed the disposable containers full of leftovers.

3.   The army was unwilling to surrender and, more importantly, to lose its country's independence.

4.   After the development of her invention, Mrs. Lopez got a promotion.

5.   The woman's utterances were so indifferent and impersonal that further discussion was impossible.

6.   Even though he was a beginner at basketball, Jason was persistent and had an expectation of perfection.

7.   Scientists have no explanation for why so many frogs and toads have a deformity.

8.   The development of the invention will reduce pollution in the community.

9.   The children seemed as if they wanted to stay at the amusement park permanently, but it was time to go home.

10.   Because of the newspaper's description of Kate, Mrs. Wood made a prediction that she would be exceptionally independent.

Lesson 19

Activity A: Vowel Combinations Review

1.	u - e	oy	or	$\boxed{\text{oo}}$	ee
2.	au	ar	e - e	er	i - e
3.	$\boxed{\text{ow}}$	oi	$\boxed{\text{ea}}$	ur	ay

Activity B: Vowel Conversions Review

i	a	o	u	e

Activity C: Prefixes and Suffixes Review

	Prefixes				
1.	im	mis	un	pre	be
2.	dis	de	con	a	en

	Suffixes				
3.	ist	ate	ic	al	sion
4.	y	ity	ant	tive	ible
5.	er	tion	ly	ness	est

Activity D: **Strategy Instruction**

1.	intolerable	combination
2.	amendment	instructional
3.	organization	understandable
4.	political	oxidize

Activity E: **Strategy Practice**

1.	reinvestigate	confident
2.	unsuspecting	government
3.	contribution	example
4.	medically	honesty
5.	executive	unspeakable

Activity F: **Word Families**

A	**B**
instruct—to teach	contribute—to give money to a charity
instructed	contributes
instructing	contributed
instructor	contributing
instruction	contributor
instructional	contributory
instructive	contribution

Activity G: **Spelling Dictation**

1.	2.
3.	4.

Activity H: **Vocabulary**

a.   not able to be tolerated (Activity D) _____

b.   able to be understood (Activity D) _____

c.   the money contributed to a charity (Activity E)

_____

Special Vocabulary

1.   amendment—When something is added to a document such as a constitution or a legal contract, the thing that is added is called an <u>amendment</u>.

2.   combination—When you put or mix several things together, the result is a <u>combination</u>.

Activity I: **Sentence Reading**

1. The enormity of the problem was both unpredictable and intolerable.

2. The complicated math example was challenging and very instructive.

3. Last week, the government passed a radical amendment to the historical law.

4. If you see your doctor regularly, many problems are medically preventable.

5. The consultant made numerous redundant suggestions to the executives.

6. By listening carefully to their utterances, you can often determine someone's honesty.

7. Because of his excellence, the employee had the distinction of getting the only promotion last year.

8. The government is going to reinvestigate the unsuspecting political organization.

9. By constantly complaining, Janet had an expectation of getting what she wanted.

10. The combination of excellence and honesty made the president of the organization an exceptional example.

Lesson 20

Activity A: Vowel Combinations Review

1.	ir	o - e	ay	oo	a - e
2.	ow	ea	oi	ou	oa

Activity B: Vowel Conversions Review

u	e	a	i	o

Activity C: Prefixes and Suffixes Review

Prefixes

1.	ad	in	com	re	pro
2.	per	a	ab	con	im

Suffixes

3.	less	ish	sive	ary	ent
4.	ance	ous	ture	able	ize
5.	or	ful	ant	age	ment

Activity D: **Strategy Instruction**

1.	persistently	governmental
2.	famously	legendary
3.	attractiveness	economize
4.	disappointment	occurrence

Activity E: **Strategy Practice**

1.	resistance	fascination
2.	unmentionable	intermission
3.	exterminate	undependable
4.	unimportance	contradiction
5.	inexpensive	invitation

Activity F: **Word Families**

A	**B**
resist—to not want to do something	attract—to bring attention to something
resisting	attracts
resister	attracted
resistive	attracting
resistible	attraction
resistibility	attractive
resistance	attractiveness

Activity G: **Spelling Dictation**

1.	2.
3.	4.

Activity H: **Vocabulary**

a.   relating to the government (Activity D)

_____

b.   something that has occurred (Activity D)

_____

c.   not able to be mentioned or talked about (Activity E)

_____

Activity I: **Passage Preparation**

Part 1—Tell

1.	nutrients	*n.*	what a plant or animal needs to stay alive
2.	nitrogen-poor	*adj.*	not having much nitrogen
*3.	dissolve	*v.*	to change a solid into a liquid
*4.	various	*adj.*	many different kinds
5.	electricity	*n.*	the power that makes appliances run
6.	electrical	*adj.*	having to do with electricity
7.	wriggles	*v.*	twists
8.	miniature	*adj.*	very small

Part 2—Strategy Practice

9.	carnivorous plants	*n.*	meat-eating plants
10.	capture	*v.*	to catch
*11.	digesting	*v.*	breaking down food so a plant or animal can use it
12.	digestive	*adj.*	related to digesting
13.	supplemental	*adj.*	extra
*14.	desperate	*adj.*	having no hope
15.	curious	*adj.*	eager to know or learn
16.	portray	*v.*	to tell about
17.	glistening	*adj.*	shining or sparkling
18.	environments	*n.*	surroundings

Activity J: **Passage Reading and Comprehension**

Meat-Eating Plants

	All plants need nutrients to stay alive, grow, and
9	reproduce. (#1) Most plants get these nutrients from the soil
18	and from the air. (#2) Some soil, however, is so nitrogen-
28	poor that plants cannot get enough nutrients. Plants that
37	live in nitrogen-poor areas sometimes get supplemental
45	nutrients from eating insects and small animals instead. We
54	call these plants **carnivorous**, or meat-eating, **plants**. (#3)
62	Carnivorous plants use various ways to attract and
70	capture the insects for food. Certain smells, bright colors
79	or patterns, or leaves covered with sparkling droplets draw
88	the insects toward them. (#4)
92	The sundew plant is a fascinating example of a
101	carnivorous plant. Tiny hairs cover the leaves of a sundew
111	plant. The hairs produce a sticky substance that clings
120	to the tips of the hairs. The sticky drops on the ends of
133	the hairs sparkle like dew in the sunlight. The glistening
143	droplets usually attract insects, such as flies. In some
152	environments, however, a sundew plant is large enough to
161	attract small animals, such as frogs. The insects or small
171	creatures approach the plant, hoping for water or food. (#5)
180	A curious fly gets too close to a sundew plant and
191	sticks to the hairs on the leaves. In a few seconds, the
203	plant traps the unsuspecting fly. When the fly wriggles and
213	tries to get away, its movement signals the sticky leaves to
224	curl tightly around it. As the leaf strangles the desperate
234	fly, the leaf pours digestive juices onto it. The juices
244	dissolve the prey, and the plant absorbs the nutrients it
254	needs. After the plant has finished digesting the fly, the leaf
265	uncurls and fills up with more sticky drops and waits for
276	its next meal. Some sundews are so sticky that people used
287	to hang them in their houses to catch flies. (#6)
296	The Venus flytrap is a legendary example of a
305	carnivorous plant. Its leaves attract insects with a sweet

314	smell, red coloring, and a broad shape that looks like a
325	good resting spot. (#7) Miniature hairs cover each leaf of
334	the plant. The moment the insect touches two or more
344	hairs, it triggers an electrical signal that tells the leaf to
355	slam shut and trap the insect. The two halves of the leaf
367	clamp together like jaws. Guard hairs along the edges of
377	the leaf prevent the insect from escaping its prison. The
387	leaf crushes the insect's body and dissolves it in order to
398	get the nutrients. (#8)
401	Although moviemakers portray carnivorous plants,
406	like the one in *Little Shop of Horrors*, as also eating
417	humans, man-eating plants don't exist in real life.
426	Fortunately for us, carnivorous plants eat only insects and
435	small animals. (#9)
437	

A. ☐   **Total number of words read**

B. ☐   **Total number of underlined words (mistakes)**

C. ☐   **Total number of words read correctly**

Lesson 21

Activity A: Vowel Combinations Review

1.	oo	oy	i - e	ai	ee
2.	e - e	or	u - e	er	ar

Activity B: Vowel Conversions Review

a	i	e	o	u

Activity C: Prefixes and Suffixes Review

Prefixes

1.	dis	be	un	ex	mis
2.	pre	de	en	ad	com

Suffixes

3.	ness	ate	ing	ist	ism
4.	ence	ous	ible	tive	y
5.	ity	est	er	le	sion

Activity D: **Strategy Instruction**

1.	unforgettable	population
2.	experimental	probably
3.	vigilant	difficulty
4.	adventurous	pilgrimage

Activity E: **Strategy Practice**

1.	dependability	incompetent
2.	disorganization	unexpectedness
3.	depression	defective
4.	unlikely	incorrectly
5.	inadmissible	prematurely

Activity F: **Word Families**

A	B
organize—to put things in order	expect—to look forward to something happening
organized	expected
organizer	expecting
organization	expectance
organizational	expectation
disorganization	unexpected
reorganize	unexpectedness

Activity G: **Spelling Dictation**

1.	2.
3.	4.

Activity H: **Vocabulary**

a.   not able to be forgotten (Activity D)

_____

b.   in a manner that is not correct (Activity E)

_____

c.   in a manner that is premature or before the best time (Activity E)

_____

Activity I: **Passage Preparation**

Part 1—Tell

1. Wilma Rudolph *n.* a woman who was a fast runner

2. pneumonia *n.* an illness

3. polio *n.* an illness that causes weakness in muscles

4. physical therapy *n.* treatment for problems in your body

5. Olympic Games *n.* sports contest among nations

6. tournament *n.* a contest involving many teams in a sport or game

*7. triumph *n.* an outstanding success

*8. obstacles *n.* things that stand in your way

Part 2—Strategy Practice

9. Tennessee *n.* a state in the United States

10. corrective *adj.* intended to correct (corrective braces)

*11. encourage *v.* to give hope and support to others

*12. persevered *v.* kept on trying to do something even if it was hard

13. determination *n.* the act of not letting anything stop you

14. decision *n.* the act of deciding or choosing something

15. American *adj.* related to the United States of America

16. international *adj.* involving more than one nation

17. foundation *n.* an organization that has money to do special things

18. inducted *v.* accepted as a member of a group or club

Activity J: **Passage Reading and Comprehension**

Wilma Rudolph, a True Hero

	Wilma Rudolph's life story is one of hope and
9	determination, adversity and triumph. She became one of
17	the most highly regarded athletes in history. (#1) The way
26	the story begins, however, does not sound like it could turn
37	out that way.
40	In 1940, Wilma was born at home, the 20th of 22
51	children. She was born prematurely and weighed only
59	4.5 pounds. Wilma soon experienced one illness after
67	another. Because of the Great Depression, Wilma's parents
75	were quite poor and could not afford medical care for her.
86	Instead, her mother took care of her. (#2)
93	She survived measles, mumps, scarlet fever, chicken
100	pox, and double pneumonia. When she was four years old,
110	her left leg was shrinking and getting weak, and Wilma's
120	mother had to take her 50 miles to visit a doctor. The doctor
133	said Wilma had polio and probably would not walk. (#3)
142	Most people would be discouraged and give up at that
152	point. Not Wilma and not Wilma's determined family! They
161	did not give up hope. After several years of hard work,
172	Wilma could walk with the aid of a metal brace.
182	Doctors also showed Wilma's mother how to do
190	physical therapy, and she showed all of Wilma's brothers
199	and sisters how to help. (#4) What happened next was
208	close to a miracle. By age 12, Wilma was walking without
219	crutches, braces, or corrective shoes. (#5)
224	Believing that sports would strengthen her leg further,
232	Wilma made a decision to become an athlete. (#6) In junior
241	high, she joined a basketball team. For three years, the
251	coach did not put her into a game. Wilma persevered,
262	however. She became a starting guard when she was in
272	tenth grade and led her team to the state championship.
282	During the tournament, the Tennessee State track coach
290	spotted her and invited her to a summer sports camp.
300	Wilma was on her way to becoming a track star. (#7)

310	When she was 16, Wilma Rudolph helped her team
319	win an Olympic medal in a relay race. Four years later,
330	Wilma became the first American woman to win three
339	gold medals in one Olympic Games. Everyone called her
348	the fastest woman in the world. She received numerous
357	awards and medals. In addition, she was inducted into the
367	Black Sports Hall of Fame, the International Sports Hall
376	of Fame, and the U.S. Olympic Hall of Fame. (#8) In 1982,
387	she started the Wilma Rudolph Foundation to encourage
395	children to overcome obstacles and follow their dreams,
403	just as her mother had taught her to do. (#9)
412	

A. ☐ **Total number of words read**

B. ☐ **Total number of underlined words (mistakes)**

C. ☐ **Total number of words read correctly**

Lesson 22

Activity A: **Vowel Combinations Review**

1.	ow	au	ay	o - e	ir
2.	ou	ea	a - e	ur	oo

Activity B: **Vowel Conversions Review**

e	o	a	u	i

Activity C: **Prefixes and Suffixes Review**

Prefixes

1.	ab	in	con	re	pro
2.	per	a	im	mis	pre

Suffixes

3.	less	ic	al	or	tion
4.	ly	ant	ance	ible	ize
5.	ture	ent	ish	age	sive

Activity D: **Strategy Practice**

1.	professionally	unfortunately
2.	exterminator	comparison
3.	instructionally	nonviolence
4.	immigration	eventually

Activity E: **Independent Strategy Practice**

1.	misinformation	enlargement
2.	communicate	conversational
3.	conditionally	accomplishment
4.	destructive	organism
5.	returnable	governmentally

Activity F: **Word Families**

A	B
inform—to tell someone something	destroy—to ruin something
informer	destruction
informant	destructive
information	destructiveness
informational	destructible
informative	indestructible
misinformation	indestructibility

Activity G: **Spelling Dictation**

1.	2.
3.	4.

Activity H: **Vocabulary**

a.	not having fortune or good luck; regretfully (Activity D)
	_____
b.	the result of accomplishing or completing something (Activity E)
	_____
c.	able to be returned (Activity E)
	_____

Activity I: **Passage Preparation**

Part 1—Tell

1.	Cesar Chavez	*n.*	a man who worked for migrant workers' rights
2.	Mexico	*n.*	a country in North America
3.	United States	*n.*	a country in North America
4.	Arizona	*n.*	a state in the United States
5.	California	*n.*	a state in the United States
6.	English	*n.*	a language
7.	believed	*v.*	accepted as true
8.	noticed	*v.*	saw something or somebody

Part 2—Strategy Practice

9.	ancestors	*n.*	people who came before us, such as our grandparents
10.	immigrate	*v.*	come into a country and settle there
*11.	migrant workers	*n.*	people who move from place to place to find work in farming
12.	vegetables	*n.*	foods such as carrots, lettuce, and beets
*13.	boycott	*n.*	a group's refusal to deal with an organization in protest
14.	supermarkets	*n.*	big grocery stores
*15.	sacrifice	*n.*	a thing given up for something of more value
*16.	nonviolent	*adj.*	not using violence or force
17.	elementary	*adj.*	referring to grades one to six
18.	attention	*n.*	the act of thinking carefully about something

Activity J: **Passage Reading and Comprehension**

Cesar Chavez, Fighter for Human Dignity

	Cesar Chavez (1927–1993) devoted his life to human
9	dignity and fairness. Throughout his life, he made
17	sacrifices so that migrant workers' lives could be better. (#1)
26	Cesar's ancestors immigrated to the United States from
34	Mexico. They left their homeland to find a better life. (#2)
44	Cesar's grandparents established a large ranch in the
52	Arizona desert and worked as farmers. Cesar was born on
62	the family ranch.
65	In 1937, when Cesar was 10 years old, the Chavez
75	family moved to California and became migrant workers.
83	"Migrant" means moving from one place to another. As
92	migrant workers, they moved from one farm to another
101	and worked for the farm owners. (#3)
107	The farm owners paid them very little to pick fruits
117	and vegetables. The migrant workers worked long hours in
126	the hot sun. Because they did not own houses, they slept
137	in small shacks that had no bathrooms, no electricity, and
147	no running water. Sometimes the shacks were so crowded,
156	they even slept in their pickup trucks. (#4)
163	Cesar said that school was very difficult for him. As
173	the families moved around, the children kept changing
181	schools. Cesar attended school sometimes for only a
189	day or two and sometimes for a few weeks or months.
200	He estimated that he went to 65 elementary schools
209	altogether! In addition, his family spoke only Spanish at
218	home, so learning to read and write English was hard for
229	him. The other students taunted (made fun of) him. (#5) In
239	spite of difficulties, Cesar was able to graduate from eighth
249	grade. Graduating was an unusual accomplishment for
256	migrant workers in those days.
261	As Cesar grew up, he noticed how difficult the migrant
271	workers' lives were. He wanted to do something about it.
281	Cesar took part in his first nonviolent protest of low wages
272	and poor working conditions by going on strike. (#6) For

301	several years, he was part of an organization called the
311	Community Service Organization. Eventually, he left to
318	form his own organization, now known as the United Farm
328	Workers (UFW).
330	Cesar Chavez and the UFW led many strikes and
339	boycotts against farm owners who refused to change the
348	working conditions. In addition, Cesar Chavez fasted, or
356	starved himself, to draw more attention to the issues. (#7)
365	People did pay attention. For example, many Americans
373	joined the boycott against table grapes. They refused to
382	buy them at their local supermarkets. The grape boycott
391	lasted for five years, but the farm owners finally made
401	some changes. (#8)
403	When Cesar Chavez died, he was 66 years old. His
413	tireless work for other people and all the fasting he did
424	were hard on his body. Nevertheless, he believed strongly
433	in making sacrifices so that other people could have better
443	lives. Today his children still work for migrant workers'
452	rights. (#9)
452	

A.	☐	**Total number of words read**
B.	☐	**Total number of underlined words (mistakes)**
C.	☐	**Total number of words read correctly**

Lesson 23

Activity A: Vowel Combinations Review

1.	or	oo	i - e	oy	ar
2.	ee	e - e	oi	ai	er

Activity B: Vowel Conversions Review

u	a	i	e	o

Activity C: Prefixes and Suffixes Review

Prefixes

1.	dis	de	un	ex	ad
2.	en	com	be	per	ab

Suffixes

3.	sive	able	ment	ful	ary
4.	le	ate	ism	ous	ence
5.	tive	ity	sion	y	er

Activity D: **Strategy Practice**

1.	reorganization	comparatively
2.	jealousy	immediately
3.	investigator	communication
4.	dissatisfaction	disadvantage

Activity E: **Independent Strategy Practice**

1.	administrative	vertically
2.	educationally	departmentally
3.	impossibility	operator
4.	completely	intentionally
5.	noisiest	discouragement

Activity F: **Word Families**

A	**B**
compare—to see how two things are alike	educate—to teach
comparison	education
comparable	educational
comparability	educationally
comparative	reeducate
comparatively	reeducating
incomparable	reeducation

Activity G: **Spelling Dictation**

1.	2.
3.	4.

Activity H: **Vocabulary**

a. the result of organizing again (Activity D)

_____

b. a person who investigates or studies (Activity D)

_____

c. in a manner that is educational (Activity E)

_____

Activity I: **Passage Preparation**

Part 1—Tell

1. *Scientific American*	*n.*	a magazine
2. Missouri	*n.*	a state in the United States
3. Minnesota	*n.*	a state in the United States
4. Australia	*n.*	a country
5. scientists	*n.*	people having knowledge of science
6. weird	*adj.*	very odd or strange
7. bizarre	*adj.*	freaky
*8. unfamiliar	*adj.*	not well known

Part 2—Strategy Practice

9. century	*n.*	100 years
10. multiple	*adj.*	many
*11. witness	*n.*	a person who saw something happen
12. incidents	*n.*	events
*13. phenomenon	*n.*	an unusual event
*14. explanation	*n.*	that which is said or written that makes something clear
15. logical	*adj.*	having to do with logic or with making sense
16. precipitation	*n.*	rain, snow, or hail
17. manufacture	*v.*	to make things with machines, usually in a factory
18. thudded	*v.*	made a heavy, dull sound

Activity J: **Passage Reading and Comprehension**

Weird Rain

9	When someone says, "It's raining cats and dogs," we don't expect to look out the window and see animals. We
20	know the person is talking about a downpour, or heavy
30	rainfall. (#1) As far as we know, no cats or dogs have
41	actually fallen from the sky. But, what if someone said it
52	was raining frogs and toads? Is that another way of saying
63	the same thing as "raining cats and dogs"? Not according
73	to multiple news accounts of unusual occurrences. (#2)
80	For more than a century, people have reported bizarre
89	incidents in which rain has included frogs, fish, or frozen
99	turtles. Try to picture in your mind what this might look
110	like. In 1873, *Scientific American* described a shower of
119	frogs that darkened the air and fell to the ground during a
131	rainstorm in Missouri. (#3) In 1901, witnesses in Minnesota
139	told a rare story. They said that they heard an unfamiliar
150	plopping outside. It sounded like falling lumps of mud,
159	not like rain or hail. Outside, they saw a huge green mass
171	coming down from the sky. When the storm was over, they
182	saw hundreds of frogs and toads piled three inches deep
192	and covering more than four blocks! (#4)
198	Many other animals have thudded to the ground
206	as well. Different kinds of fish have fallen on priests in
217	Australia, golfers in England, and families in Singapore.
225	Sometimes birds frozen like hailstones have dropped to
233	the earth. In 1930, *Nature* magazine told a story about a
244	turtle wrapped in ice that fell during a hailstorm. (#5)
253	How does this strange precipitation happen? Some
260	scientists believe they have a logical explanation for the
269	weird rain or hail. They tell us that a violent thunderstorm
280	picks up animals from shallow ponds or creeks and pulls
290	the animals high into the air. Then these whirlwinds carry
300	the animals for hundreds of miles before throwing them
309	to the ground. They compare this phenomenon to what

318	happens in dry areas where huge, whirling dust storms are
328	constantly dropping rubbish out of the sky. (#6)
335	Other scientists say that we don't really know how
344	weird rain happens. In another odd event, however, a
353	tornado dropped unopened soft drink cans. The cans were
362	marked with the name of the manufacturing plant. The
371	plant was 150 miles away from where the full cans landed.
382	Whether the logical explanations are proved or not, let's
391	hope the weatherperson doesn't start predicting soft drink
399	showers for tomorrow's weather. (#7)
403	

A. ☐ **Total number of words read**

B. ☐ **Total number of underlined words (mistakes)**

C. ☐ **Total number of words read correctly**

Lesson 24

Activity A: **Vowel Combinations Review**

1.	u - e	ea	au	oa	o - e
2.	ay	ou	oo	ow	ur

Activity B: **Vowel Conversions Review**

o	i	e	u	a

Activity C: **Prefixes and Suffixes Review**

		Prefixes			
1.	mis	in	con	pre	pro
2.	a	im	re	com	ad

		Suffixes			
3.	ness	ing	ist	est	ant
4.	ance	ture	ible	ize	ent
5.	sive	ish	al	or	tion

Activity D: **Strategy Practice**

1.	productivity	escalator
2.	unmistakable	imperfectly
3.	tantalize	redundantly
4.	unavoidable	unmanageable

Activity E: **Independent Strategy Practice**

1.	unattractiveness	exceptionality
2.	preparation	disagreements
3.	meaningfulness	publicize
4.	dramatically	radiant
5.	inconsistence	reactionary

Activity F: **Word Families**

A	**B**
continue—to keep doing something	consist—to be made up of
continued	consistent
continuing	consistently
continuation	consistence
continual	consistency
continually	inconsistent
continuous	inconsistence

Activity G: **Spelling Dictation**

1.	2.
3.	4.

Activity H: **Vocabulary**

a.	the state of being productive or making a lot (Activity D)
b.	not able to be managed or controlled (Activity D)
c.	the act of preparing something or making something ready for use (Activity E)

Activity I: **Passage Preparation**

Part 1—Tell

*1. record
     breaker   *n.*   someone or something that beats a
                                previous record

2.   measured   *v.*   figured out the amount in inches,
                                meters, miles, etc.

3.   koala bear   *n.*   an animal of Australia

4.   eucalyptus   *n.*   a tree of Australia

5.   Galapagos   *n.*   islands of South America
     Islands

6.   tortoise   *n.*   a turtle

7.   endangered   *n.*   a species of animal or plant that
     species   may die out

8.   Thailand   *n.*   a country

Part 2—Strategy Practice

9.   explorers   *n.*   people who travel to new places to
                                learn about them

*10. category   *n.*   a group of ideas or things

*11. feature   *n.*   a distinct part of something, such
                                as a part of your face

12. imaginable   *adj.*   able to be imagined

13. contrast   *n.*   a difference

*14. amazing   *adj.*   surprising

15. hibernate   *v.*   to sleep through the winter

16. caterpillar   *n.*   wormlike animal that becomes a
                                butterfly or moth

17. multitude   *n.*   a very large number of people or things

18. host   *n.*   a very large number of people or things

Activity J: **Passage Reading and Comprehension**

Record Breakers in the Animal World

	In the animal world, record breakers exist in every
9	category imaginable. People could tell you which animal
17	is the biggest, the tallest, the smallest, and the heaviest of
28	all animals. People could tell you which animal is fussiest,
38	hungriest, thirstiest, and quietest. Animals hold records
45	for shouting the loudest, diving the deepest, hibernating
53	the longest, and digging the biggest burrows. (#1)
60	Record breakers in the animal world live on every
69	continent on earth. Some live on only one continent, and
79	some live on every continent. The fussiest eater, the koala
89	bear, lives only in Australia. (#2) Even though more than
98	100 types of eucalyptus trees grow in Australia, the koala
108	bear eats leaves from only 12 types. In fact, the koala
119	bear is so fussy, it cannot eat anything except eucalyptus
129	leaves. (#3)
130	The hungriest animal on earth lives on all continents.
139	Perhaps you have heard of the hungry caterpillar. It eats
149	constantly. From the time it hatches until it turns into a
160	butterfly, it eats so much that its weight can increase as
171	much as 3,000 times. (#4)
175	The longest earthworm in the world lives in southern
184	Africa. Someone actually measured the biggest one he or
193	she found, and it was more than 6 meters (20 feet) long.
205	That is longer than three tall men lying on the ground head
217	to toe. (#5)
219	In contrast, the world's smallest mammal is no bigger
228	than a human's thumb. Thailand's bumblebee bat weighs
236	less than a penny. Bumblebee bats are one of the 12 most
248	endangered species. At last count, the Thai government
256	could find only 160. (#6)
260	A multitude of howler monkeys still exist, though, in
269	Central and South America. The male howlers have the
278	distinction of being the world's noisiest land animal.

286	A special box in their throat makes their shouts so loud,
297	they can be heard almost 10 miles away! (#7)
305	The tortoise that lives on the Galapagos Islands is the
315	largest tortoise found anywhere. (#8) The word *galápago*
322	is Spanish for "tortoise," which is why explorers gave the
332	islands that name. A mature Galapagos tortoise can weigh
341	as much as 700 pounds, measure 4 feet in length, and live
353	as long as 200 years. (#9)
358	Most humans never tire of finding out which animals
367	break records for speed, size, amount they eat or drink,
377	number of offspring they bring into the world at one time,
388	or a host of other animal features. Whether they are the
399	oldest, loudest, or most endangered, animals are quite
407	amazing. (#10)
408	

A. ☐ **Total number of words read**

B. ☐ **Total number of underlined words (mistakes)**

C. ☐ **Total number of words read correctly**

Lesson 25

Activity A: **Vowel Combinations Review**

1.	a - e	oo	i - e	ir	oy
2.	ee	ai	ar	or	ow

Activity B: **Vowel Conversions Review**

a	u	i	e	o

Activity C: **Prefixes and Suffixes Review**

Prefixes

1.	un	dis	per	en	ex
2.	ab	com	de	con	be

Suffixes

3.	less	ic	ful	sion	tive
4.	y	ment	ly	ous	able
5.	ate	ism	age	ary	ence

Activity D: **Strategy Practice**

1.	unrepairable	respectability
2.	individuality	occasionally
3.	mismanagement	generosity
4.	environmentally	disappearance

Activity E: **Independent Strategy Practice**

1.	competition	tremendously
2.	instrumentalist	superintendent
3.	additionally	dissimilarity
4.	impracticality	fundamentally
5.	indescribable	unconventionality

Activity F: **Word Families**

A	**B**
manage—to tell a group what to do	appear—to come into sight
manager	appearance
management	disappear
manageable	disappears
mismanage	disappearing
mismanaged	disappearance
unmanageable	disappearances

Activity G: **Spelling Dictation**

1.	2.
3.	4.

Activity H: **Vocabulary**

a.	not able to be repaired or fixed (Activity D)
b.	someone who makes music on an instrument (Activity E)
c.	not able to be described (Activity E)

Activity I: **Passage Preparation**

Part 1—Tell

1.	Soviet Union	*n.*	the name of a former country
2.	Russian	*adj.*	related to the country of Russia
3.	cosmonaut	*n.*	a Russian astronaut
4.	Laika	*n.*	the name of a dog that went into space
*5.	knowledge	*n.*	facts that have been learned
6.	atmosphere	*n.*	the air above the earth
7.	species	*n.*	a specific kind of plant or animal
8.	medicines	*n.*	drugs used to treat diseases

Part 2—Strategy Practice

9.	vertical	*adj.*	standing or pointing straight up
10.	capsule	*n.*	a closed container
11.	researchers	*n.*	people who study something
12.	monument	*n.*	a building or statue built in memory of a person or event
13.	memorial	*n.*	something in memory of a person or event including a monument
*14.	monitor	*v.*	to keep a close watch on
*15.	respond	*v.*	to give an answer
*16.	resemble	*v.*	to look like
17.	good-natured	*adj.*	nice; easygoing
18.	weightlessness	*n.*	the state of having little or no weight—especially when out in space

Activity J: **Passage Reading and Comprehension**

Animals in Space

	Before the first humans blasted into space, animals
8	became the first astronauts. Beginning in the 1940s,
16	humans sent many kinds of animals into space, including
25	monkeys, dogs, cats, fish, frogs, and many other species.
34	(#1) Scientists used the animals to study many aspects
42	of space travel to prepare for the first human flight. For
53	example, the animals tested what it was like to travel in
64	small space capsules. The animals helped identify possible
72	dangers to humans and taught humans important things
80	about how to live and work in space. (#2)
88	One of the most famous animal astronauts was
96	Laika, the dog. She was the first living creature to leave
107	the earth's atmosphere and orbit the earth. Laika was a
117	mongrel, or mutt, with no owner or home and lived on
128	the streets of Moscow. Suddenly, some Soviet researchers
136	captured her. They took her to a Soviet research center
146	and promoted her to the rank of cosmonaut, the name that
157	the Soviet Union uses for its astronauts. (#3)
164	Laika, a good-natured dog, responded well to her
173	spaceflight training. She learned to live and sleep while
182	wearing a special harness. She also learned to eat and drink
193	from special containers prepared just for her flight. (#4)
201	Laika's cabin resembled an egg-shaped nest. Soft
209	padded fabric covered the vertical walls of the cabin.
218	Measuring tools filled every nook and cranny of her
227	new home.
229	On November 5, 1957, Laika's spacecraft, *Sputnik 2*,
237	was launched into space. While Laika traveled around the
246	earth, scientists monitored her heartbeat, blood pressure,
253	and breathing rate. They hoped to learn how humans
262	might behave on future spaceflights. Laika helped humans
270	answer questions about the effects of escaping the earth's
279	atmosphere, living in such a small space, and how a body
290	would respond to weightlessness. (#5)

294	Today, more than 40 years after Laika's spaceflight,
302	her statue is part of a monument to Russian cosmonauts
312	that stands outside of Moscow. Laika is the only animal
322	that is part of the memorial. Some people consider her
332	contribution to science to be as important as that of any
343	human astronaut.
345	Animals are still going into orbit. All kinds of birds,
355	insects, and animals, even 2,000 jellyfish, have gone
363	into space. Animals in outer space contribute to new
372	understandings about the human body, disease prevention,
379	and the development of medicines. Animals in space help
388	humans understand life, growth, and development. This
395	research adds to our knowledge of humans, animals, and
404	every aspect of our planet. (#6)
409	

A. ☐ **Total number of words read**

B. ☐ **Total number of underlined words (mistakes)**

C. ☐ **Total number of words read correctly**

Strategies for Reading Long Words

Overt Strategy

1. Circle the prefixes.

2. Circle the suffixes.

3. Underline the vowels.

4. Say the parts of the word.

5. Say the whole word.

6. Make it a real word.

EXAMPLE

Covert Strategy

1. Look for prefixes, suffixes, and vowels.

2. Say the parts of the word.

3. Say the whole word.

4. Make it a real word.

Prefixes, Suffixes, and Vowel Combinations

	Decoding Element	Key Word	Decoding Element	Key Word	Decoding Element	Key Word
Prefixes	a	above	de	depart	mis	mistake
	ab	absent	dis	disagree	per	permit
	ad	addition	en	enlist	pre	prevent
	be	belong	ex	export	pro	protect
	com	compare	im	immature	re	return
	con	continue	in	incomplete	un	unfair
Suffixes	able	comfortable	ful	careful	ment	argument
	age	courage	ible	reversible	ness	kindness
	al	final	ic	athletic	or	tailor
	ance	disturbance	ing	running	ous	famous
	ant	dormant	ish	selfish	s	birds
	ary	missionary	ism	realism	sion	discussion
	ate	regulate	ist	artist	sive	expensive
	ed	landed	ity	oddity	tion	action
	ence	influence	ize	memorize	tive	attentive
	ent	persistent	le	cradle	ture	picture
	er	farmer	less	useless	y	thirsty
	est	biggest	ly	safely		
Vowel Combinations	ai	rain	oo	moon, book	or	torn
	au	sauce	ou	loud	ur	turn
	ay	say	ow	low, down	a-e	make
	ea	meat, thread	oy	boy	e-e	Pete
	ee	deep	ar	farm	i-e	side
	oa	boat	er	her	o-e	hope
	oi	boil	ir	bird	u-e	use

REWARDS Chart

Name _____

Lesson	First Page Activities A, B, C, D	Second Page Activities E, F, and G	Third Page Activities H, I, and J	Reading Check Line in H	Bonus Points	Total Points	Lesson Grade
Lesson 1							
Lesson 2							
Lesson 3							
Lesson 4							
Lesson 5							
Lesson 6							
Lesson 7							
Lesson 8							
Lesson 9							
Lesson 10							
Lesson 11							
Lesson 12							
Lesson 13							
Lesson 14							
Lesson 15							
Lesson	First Page Activities A, B, and C	Second Page Activities D, E, and F	Third Page Activities G and H	Reading Check Sentence in I	Bonus Points	Total Points	Lesson Grade
Lesson 16							
Lesson 17							
Lesson 18							
Lesson 19							
Lesson	First Page Activities A, B, and C	Second Page Activities D, E, and F	Third Page Activities G and H	Fluency Check Passage in J	Bonus Points	Total Points	Lesson Grade
Lesson 20							
Lesson 21							
Lesson 22							
Lesson 23							
Lesson 24							
Lesson 25							

Participation Points (3 possible points)
- Following behavioral guidelines
- Paying attention and participating
- Responding accurately

Fluency Check
100–150 CWPM* = 3 points
80–99 CWPM = 2 points
60–79 CWPM = 1 point

* CWPM = correct words per minute

Reading Check (line or sentence)
No errors = 3 points
1 error = 2 points
2 errors = 1 point

Lesson Grade (12 possible points)
11 or 12 points = A
9 or 10 points = B
7 or 8 points = C
5 or 6 points = D
Fewer than 6 = F

Total Points	Overall Grade

Name _____

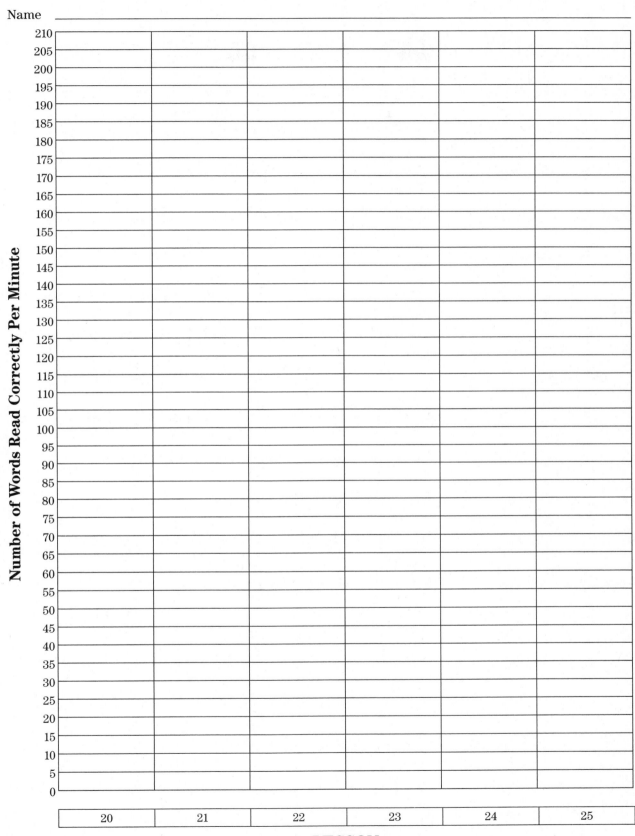

Number of Words Read Correctly Per Minute

| | 20 | 21 | 22 | 23 | 24 | 25 |

LESSON